Sensual
Swimwear

Text and Captions
Roger Baker

Photography
Peter Barry, Colour Library Books,
John Kelly, Neal Peters Collection,
The Photographers' Library,
PictureBank, Peter Pugh-Cook,
The Telegraph Colour Library

Design
Philip Clucas, MSIAD

CLB 2747
© 1991 Colour Library Books Ltd., Godalming, Surrey, England.
All rights reserved.
This 1991 edition published by Crescent Books,
distributed by Outlet Book Company, Inc.,
a Random House Company,
225 Park Avenue South, New York, New York 10003.
Printed and bound in Singapore.
ISBN 0 517 06546 0
8 7 6 5 4 3 2 1

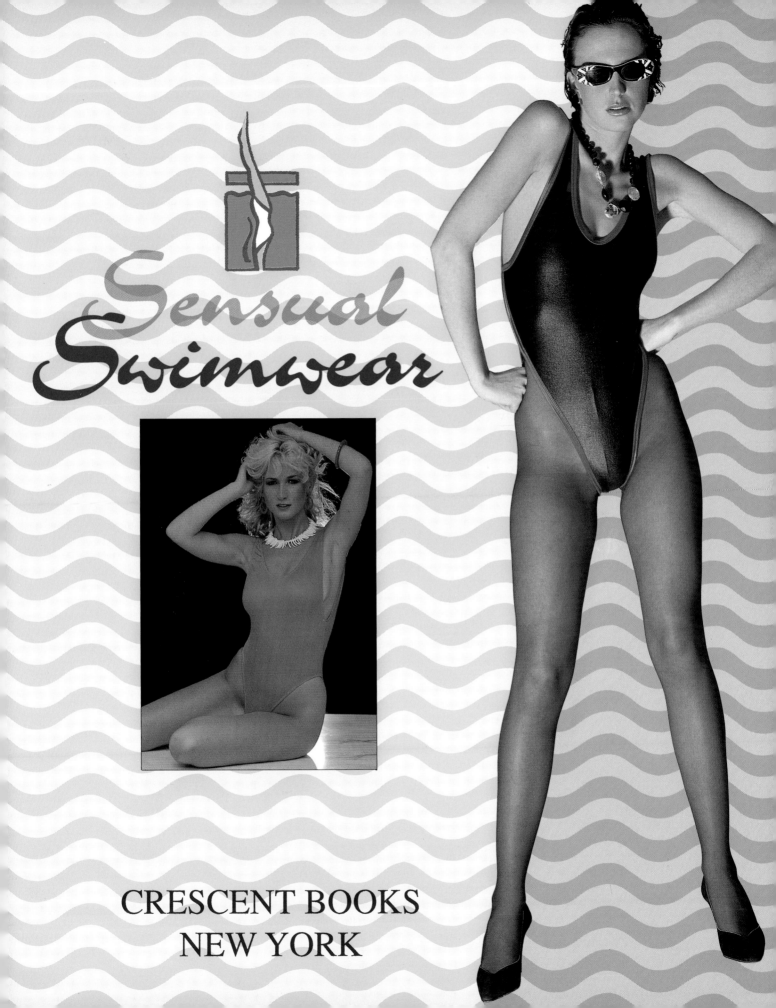

Sensual Swimwear

CRESCENT BOOKS
NEW YORK

Sensual Swimwear

Introduction

Swimwear is one of the great inventions of our times. Decorative as well as practical, in many ways it symbolizes the great social changes that characterized the second quarter of the twentieth century. After the massive upheaval of the First World War, two new themes emerged in Europe and America: the increasing independence of women, and a growing enthusiasm for health and fitness. At one extreme this led to naturism. More commonly, countless men and women responded to the attractions of open-air sports and the much-promoted benefits of sea-bathing by demanding appropriate garments that coupled practicality with modesty.

One of the great early pioneers of sea-bathing was Madame Curie, twice a Nobel prize winner. She rejected the fashionable costumes of the time, with their almost ankle-length bloomers, frills, ribbons and lace, and opted for much simpler wear, thereby setting international trends.

By the 1920s, women's swimwear was beginning to take on the shape and cut which is familiar today. However, although one-piece suits were now comparatively brief and figure-hugging, modesty prevailed, and they ended perhaps one third of the way down the thigh, giving the effect of shorts. The first backless bathing costumes appeared in 1930 and, by the end of the decade, windows were being cut in the center front of the garment to reveal a triangle or circle of bare skin - just one step away from the ultimate separation of the costume into two pieces.

During this period two other elements influenced the evolution of swimwear: fashion and glamour. Rich socialites parading at smart resorts on Long Island or in the south of France made the simple bathing costume a fashion item in its own right, something to be worn with full make-up and handsome jewelry – making it more suitable for diving into a Martini than the Mediterranean. In addition, swimwear became standard wear for Hollywood pinups such as Betty Grable (facing page).

Introduction

There are few garments that flatter a superb figure more than a bathing costume – nor does it have to be elaborate. Two great glamour stars, Jayne Mansfield (below) and Elizabeth Taylor (right) found a simple one-piece quite adequate.

Sensual Swimwear

All at Sea

When it comes to messing about in boats, girls today are no longer happy to lie back with a drink and watch their boyfriends do all the work. Brimming with health and vitality, they too want to haul on the ropes, unfurl the sails and climb the ladders, while the sun and salt spray slowly turn their skin to shades of gold.

They want practical clothes to do all this in, but these clothes have to be attractive and flattering as well, allowing maximum ease of movement and maximum exposure to the sun. For some, the briefest of briefs and the tiniest of tops are sufficient, with the addition of a loose shirt to throw on for protection when the afternoon sun gets too hot. For others, a sleek one-piece suit fits the bill.

Not only are yachting holidays never predictable but no two are ever the same, whether they take place among the picturesque coves of the Italian islands or under the gently swaying palms of Hawaii. Moments of brisk activity can be followed by periods of indolence, when there is nothing more to do than to rest on deck, relaxing and sunbathing as the boat lies motionless in a calm sea.

There may be a picnic on deck, followed by an urge to dive overboard, and swim among coral reefs, chase dolphins or simply float dreamily in the warm, caressing water. The right clothes make it all possible.

Later, as the sun begins to sink and velvety dusk envelops the earth, there is still no need to change: the air is still warm and a swimsuit, perhaps with the addition of a colorful jacket or shirt, flatters long legs and glowing skin. Later still, when the stars are twinkling high above and colored lights glitter around the harbor, a stroll along the quayside brings another perfect day to a perfect end.

All at Sea

Brilliant colors and a stylish cut add glamour and allure to a boat's crew - and no sensible crew member is ever without a life jacket!

All at Sea

Whether blown by the wind, lapped by the water, or simply stuck on the land, today's bathing belle has plenty of stunning outfits to choose from.

Sensual Swimwear

Pretty Pastels

Sunworshippers, stretched on the baked terracotta tiles beside a swimming pool, or on the fine golden sand, or on the bleached rocks of a secluded beach, sport a dazzling array of costumes in every shade from a challenging turquoise through to the pale aqua of the water itself.

Color is important; it reflects not only a girl's character and taste, but also the way in which she sees herself and would like others to see her. Scarlet, black and white can be dramatic, suggesting enthusiasm, and a zest for the sharper edge of life. More subtle pastel shades suggest a softer, gentler and more feminine side. Most feminine of all is pink, traditional color of girlhood.

Cut is important too. The earliest swimwear was essentially practical, designed for swimmers who wanted something plain and serviceable. When it became clear that the swimming costume had the potential to be a fashionable and glamourous item, however, the designers stepped in to vary its color and cut. The earliest Hollywood pinup shots show the superstars in simple, plain-colored one-piece suits. But they still had impact, if only in the way the garment was cut to flatter the contours of the body.

Throughout the 1930s more and more people in the vast, expanding industrial cities of America and Europe began to spend their weekends and holidays beside the sea. New Yorkers would rush to spend a day on the happy but overcrowded beaches of Coney Island. Those living far from the sea would gather at one of the local public pools, or – if they were very lucky – around the private pools which had become a feature of well-heeled suburban life. The swimming costume became an important item in any girl's wardrobe and the availability of inexpensive, off-the-peg swimsuits from local chain stores brought the alluring look of the Hollywood stars within reach of everybody. So swimwear grew in popularity and, on summer weekends, the girls soaking up the sunshine on lawns and verandahs resembled a border of brilliant flowers in their multi-colored swimwear.

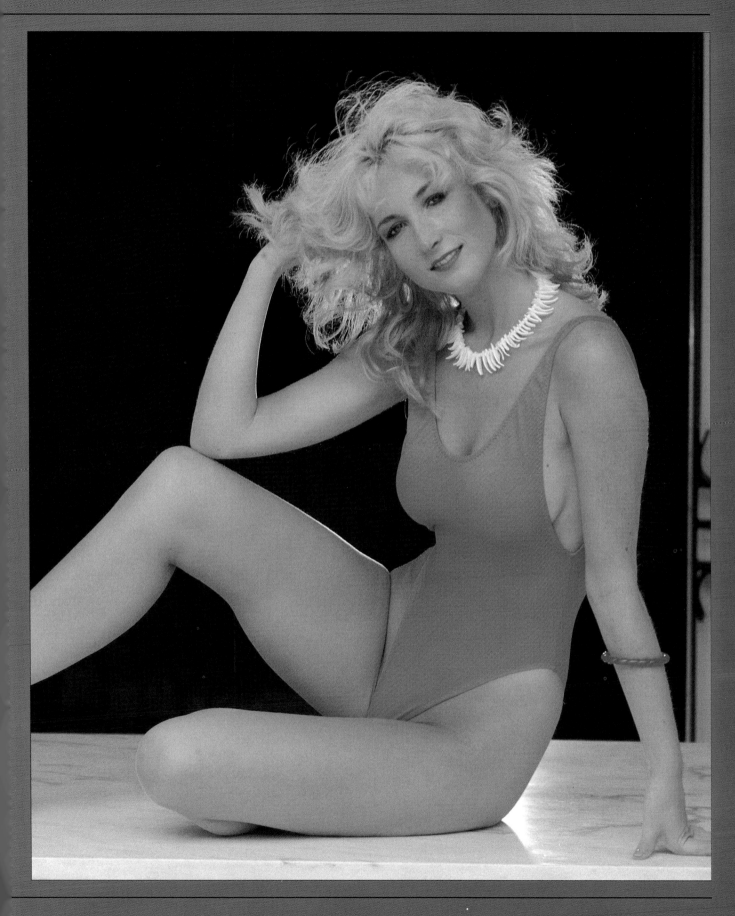

Pretty Pastels

Pink takes on an extra resonance when seen against the dramatic backdrop of either a tropical blue sky, or lush green foliage or silvery sand and glows like a rare, and exotic flower.

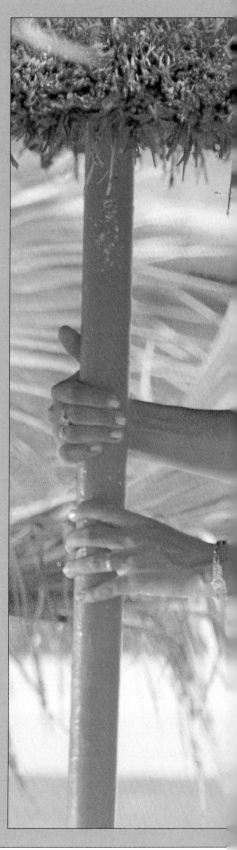

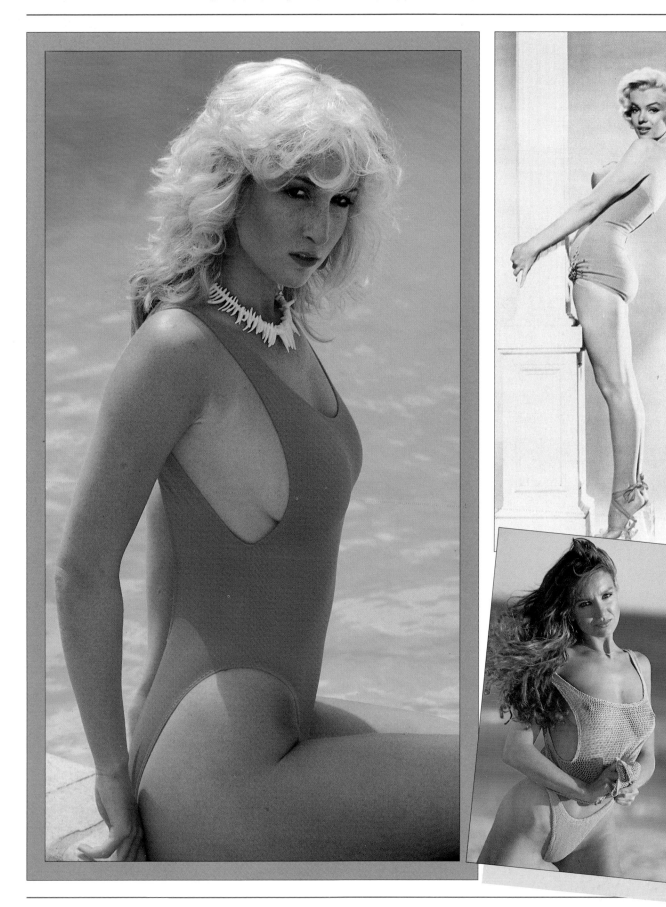

*Pretty
Pastels*

Pretty Pastels

Sensual Swimwear

Taking the Plunge

"Wet, she was a star!" was Joe Pasternak's famous put-down of the glamorous swimming personality Esther Williams. He was suggesting that her acting wasn't all that hot, but he did have a point – a beautiful girl emerging wet from the sea, the pool or even the shower seems to transcend the ordinary and become something mythical, like a mermaid. Small wonder that, over the years, some of the most memorable pinup photographs have depicted the stars coming, like Venus, out of the sea. The classic photograph of Raquel Welch on page thirty-nine illustrates the point.

Ms Welch's brief two-piece costume in that photograph tells us a great deal about the evolution of swimwear this century. Less than a hundred years ago, women who wanted to risk dipping their toes in the sea dressed up, rather than down, for the occasion, donning long pantaloons that reached to the ankle, and big blouses with huge sleeves, all decorated with ribbons and bows. More than that, cumbersome bathing machines carried them right down to the water's edge so that they were spared the immodesty of walking across a public beach.

It was the gradual emancipation of women, plus a recognition of the health-giving properties of sun- and sea-bathing that transformed swimwear into something more practical, more decorative and, slowly, ever more minimal, as women everywhere aimed to achieve the deepest, most extensive tan possible. Yet, at one time, it was considered very bad form for any woman (or man) to sport a tan – it suggested they worked in the open air! A clear pale skin was a sign of money, class and breeding. The healthy lure of the sun and the sea eventually put paid to that view and the egalitarian nature of swimwear triumphed. For the shopgirl and the countess had equal access to the sun and a golden tan was a glamorous asset available to all.

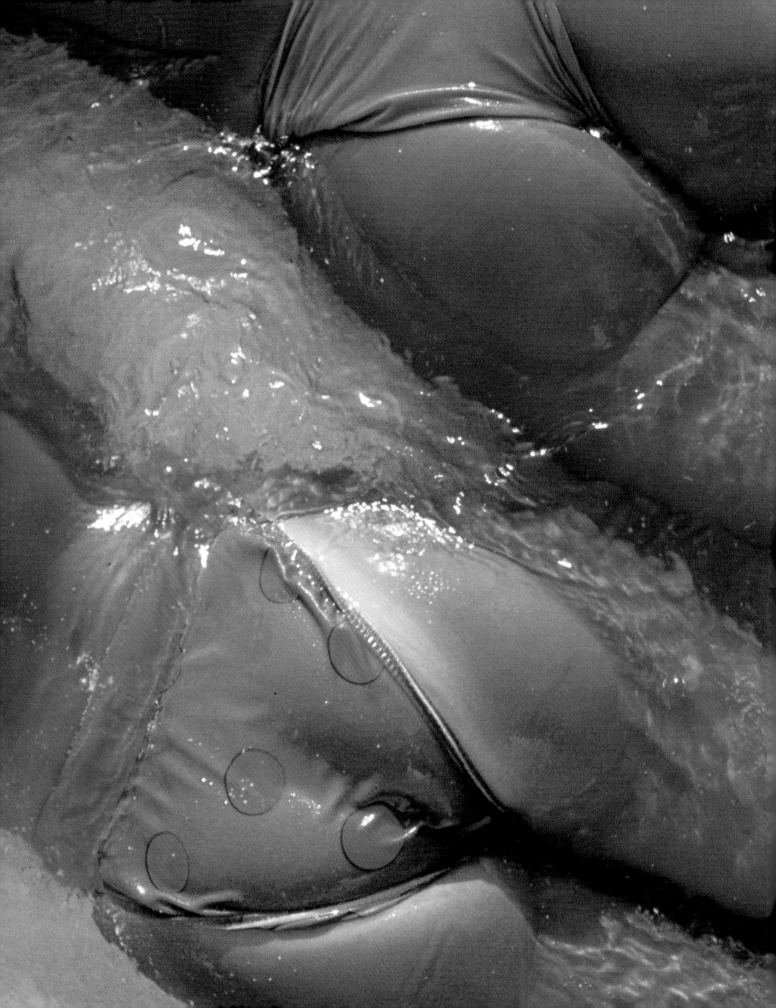

Taking the Plunge

The invigorating effects of sun and
water can increase vitality, and
bring a new energy, a new pulse
to life. Biologists may be able to
provide scientific reasons for this,
but who needs them when the
exuberance and joy are so easy
to see?

Taking the Plunge

Taking the Plunge

There are those who relax by just watching the water and those who like the water to take a more active part in washing away the cares of the day. Similarly, while some wade out to meet the sea, others prefer to lie languorously on the beach and let the sea come to them.

Taking the Plunge

Along the coasts of California, France and Australia giant breakers entice the surfer to dramatic feats, but many prefer a more passive approach to the waves. Whatever its source, the stimulating effect of water on the skin is always therapeutic.

Sensual Swimwear

Animal Magnetism

When Ava Gardner posed for the justly famous pinup photograph on the facing page, she was the reigning glamour goddess at the MGM studios. Although she is wearing a classic one-piece bathing costume, her impeccable make-up, beautifully styled hair and dramatic costume jewelry make it clear the photo session was not to be followed by a quick swim in the nearest pool.

Whenever Hollywood wanted to suggest the dangerous allure of the femme fatale, it reached for a leopard skin. The reasoning was that the audience would attribute the slinky grace and lethal potential of the animal itself to the person wearing a reproduction of its skin. Materials printed with leopard or tiger-skin patterns have been used with both subtlety and obviousness in this context since movies began. To signal that a woman had changed from prim and proper to predatory, she would be costumed in an appropriate animal-skin print. For the dream sequence in *The Seven Year Itch*, Marilyn Monroe was given a tiger-striped sheath to wear to emphasize her transformation.

The woman who chooses an animal-skin pattern to wear is making a definite statement about herself; she is associating herself with the characteristics of the big cats: quiet stealth, sinuous elegance, sudden pounce and, above all, feline beauty. For daytime outfits, the patterns may be used in incidental or purely decorative ways – for a belt, a collar and hat, or perhaps a pair of boots. In the fashion trade such a look is called *sauvage*.

For swimwear, however, it is easy to create a complete garment that seems to impart all those animal characteristics to the wearer, so that, in some mysterious way, woman and cat become almost as one.

Animal Magnetism

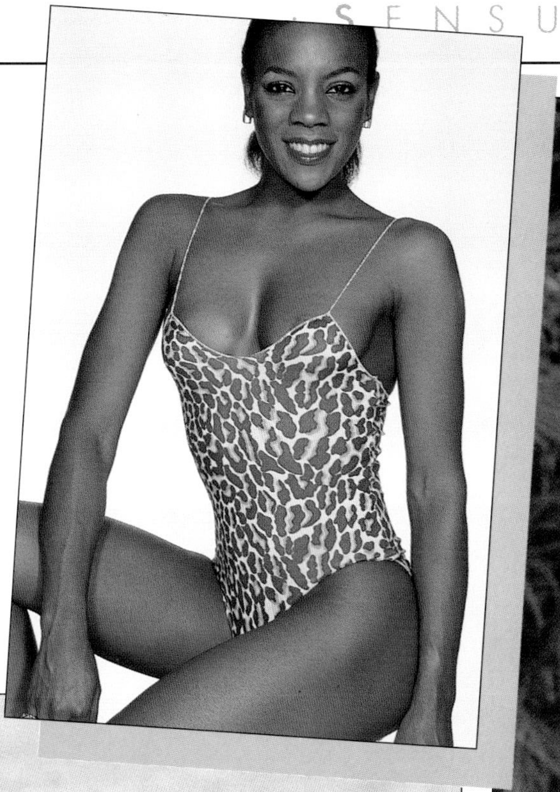

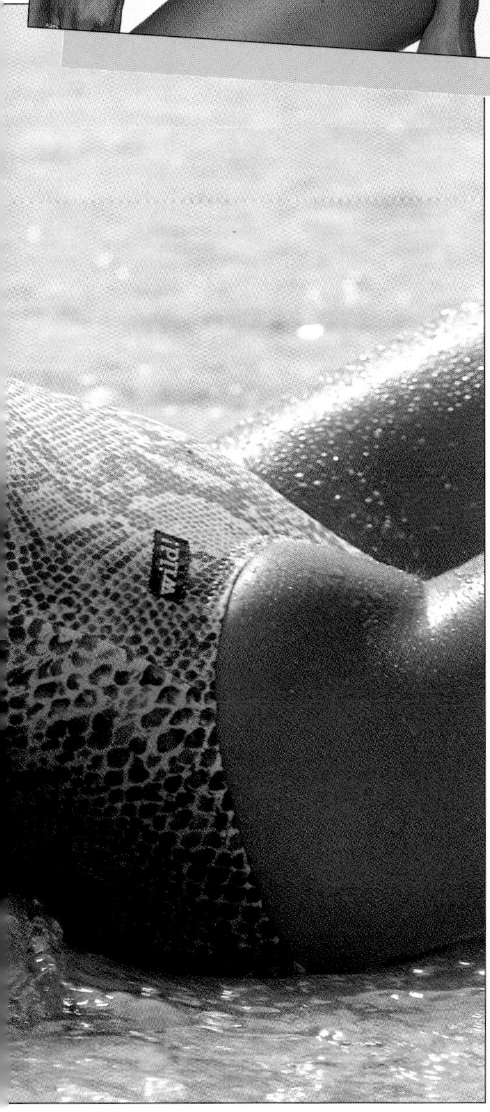

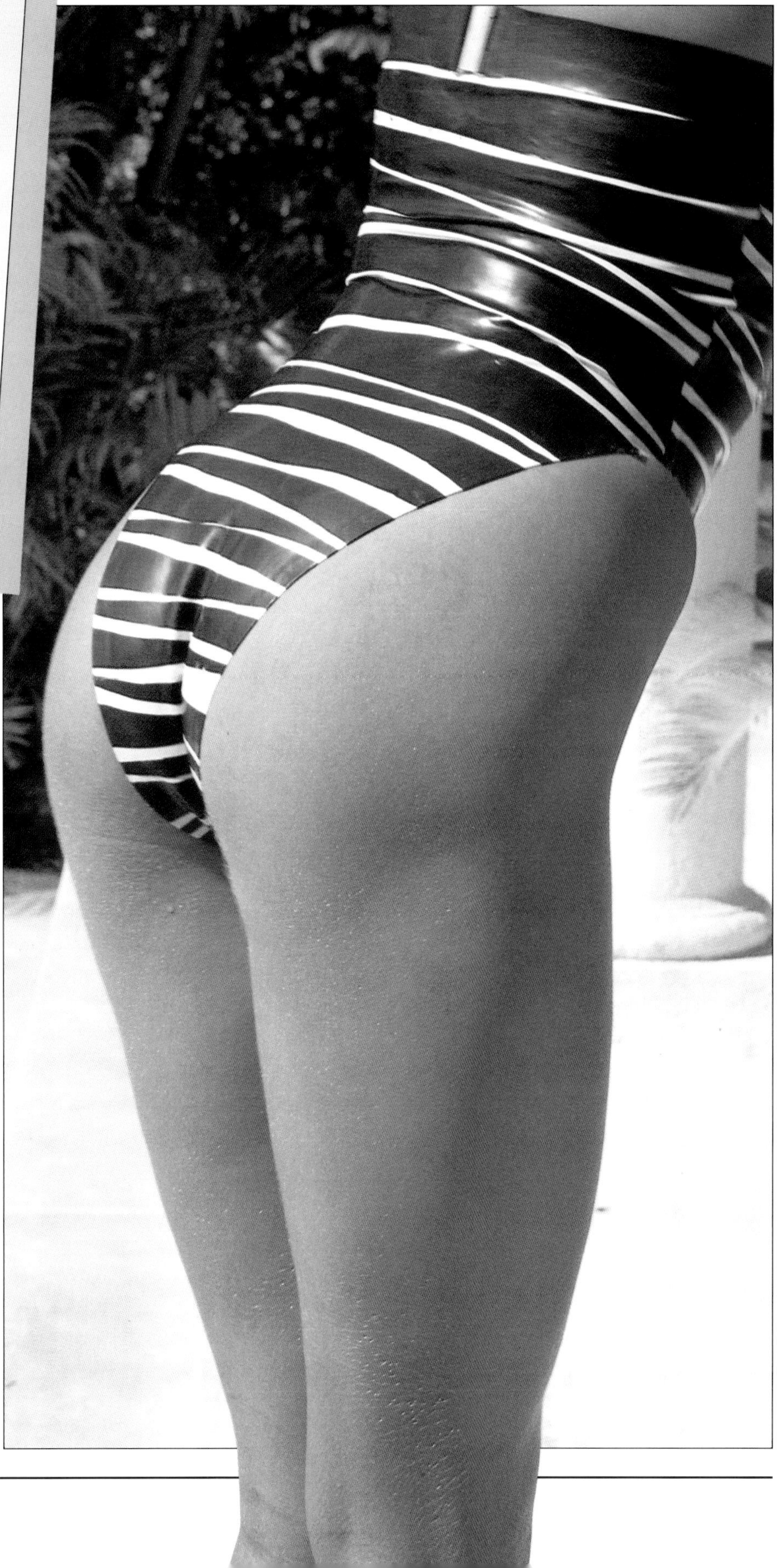

Animal Magnetism

In a tropical paradise, animal-skin prints provide a touch of exotic drama that goes perfectly with white sand and blue seas – and in the interests of conservation, beach and waterside prowlers flaunt synthetic fabrics that suggest danger without endangering the jungle cats.

Sensual Swimwear

Polka Dots and Stripes

By the 1950s, a swimming costume had become an essential part of every young woman's wardrobe – whether she could swim or not. The restrictions of the immediate postwar period had vanished and there was a new spirit of abundance, giving apparently limitless choice in everything from food to clothes. Science was evolving completely new ranges of man-made fibers, many of which were perfect for the creation of form-fitting, fine-quality swimwear.

Young people had never before had so many opportunities for enjoying themselves. Beach and pool parties were particularly popular and pretty swimwear was an essential ingredient. Also, the young people of the western world were on the move. Foreign holidays could be taken relatively inexpensively, as air travel brought other countries within easy reach.

Other restrictions were being relaxed as well – notably just how much of the body could be revealed on the beach. The swimsuit had already split into two parts, but, as can be seen in an early swimwear pose of the young Marilyn Monroe on page fifty-three, these early two-piece suits were still distinctly decorous, with the navel remaining firmly covered up.

Not for long! Briefs became briefer and tops became tinier; and designers, from those of the exclusive salons of Europe to the chain-store mass producers, extended their imaginations almost limitlessly to create swimwear in a dazzling range of color, pattern, and style. The wearer's choice of pattern always tells us something about her character. Like a streak of lightning, stripes suggest activity, speed, and energy, whether cutting through the water or on land. Polka dots are playful, girlish, fun; they suggest freshness and innocence, and have an adolescent charm. A popular song of the fifties had the refrain: "She wore an itsy-bitsy, teeny-weeny, yellow polka dot bikini ..." Swimwear had reached its most daring design yet.

The new, ever briefer swimwear was enthusiastically espoused by a rising generation of big, blond bombshells from Marilyn Monroe to Mamie van Doren – publicity photos had come a long way since the days of Betty Grable!

Polka Dots and Stripes

Jayne Mansfield (left), outgoing, witty and exuberant, appeared destined to take over the pedestal occupied by Marilyn Monroe. Destiny wrote otherwise, but before her untimely death, Mansfield had created her own image in studio sessions such as this one. Although remaining well within the bounds of discretion, the flattering, polka-dot swimsuit was cut rather daringly high in the leg for its period.

Sea Green-Ocean Blue

The combination of woman and water creates a powerful image that is fascinating, disturbing and elusive. It is no accident that Venus, the Goddess of Love herself, is often depicted at the moment of her birth, rising naked from the sea, riding on a sea shell and attended by her maidens. Ancient stories of mermaids and water sprites abound - even in those countries that have no coastline; rivers, waterfalls and deep dark pools contain their own mystery.

The Lorelei and the Greek sirens lure sailors to a rocky death with their singing; there are maidens guarding the gold at the bottom of the River Rhine, teasing and tantalizing the foolish men who dare to try and steal it from them. From time to time sad sprites fall in love with mortal men, but they always have to return, alone, to their shady green homes beneath the waves; and both Shakespeare and Ibsen created heroines who emerge from the sea to create havoc among the men they meet. Maybe such creatures really exist; if they do not, our imagination obviously needs to create them.

Water can be a potent metaphor for the strength, the flexibility, the joyous abandon, the tantalizing elusiveness and the danger that are all part of woman herself. By diving into the curling waves and disappearing beneath the water's surface, woman ceases to be an ordinary, earth-bound creature and becomes one with another element, achieving an almost mythical dimension.

The colors that water assumes reflect these romantic, other-worldly moods. Seas and oceans may mirror the intense azure of tropical skies, or the cooler blues of more northern climes; rivers and pools absorb the changeable greens of leaves and grass. In the depths of both, the colors darken around the tendrils of the plants that grow suspended there. Blues and greens are more subtly suggestive than the hot tones of scarlet and orange. Girls playing by the shore in their sea-green and ocean-blue swimwear may represent a modern, youthful exuberance, but they also subtly recall the mystery of ancient legends.

Sea Green - Ocean Blue

In a classic study, Marilyn Monroe (far right) poses in a sea-green swimsuit, and the fantasy mermaid of a million dreamers assumes a potent, human form.

Sensual Swimwear

Bare Essentials

There is a cartoon which shows a young man and his girlfriend walking hand in hand along a beach. They are passed by a pretty girl and the young man turns around to take another look at her. The joke is that, while the young man's girl is completely naked, the one he is staring at is wearing a brief two-piece swimming costume, making the point that the body which is covered – however briefly – has more sensual appeal than total nudity.

Which explains why, although an "anything goes" approach applies to today's swimwear, total nudity is still a rare sight on most beaches. Naturists may be making a deliberate statement about themselves but most people seem to prefer minimal cover-up to total exposure. Over the years swimwear has been gradually evolving toward the former; neck to ankle cover became mid-thigh to shoulder; the slinkier one-piece bathing suit became the divided two-piece. However, the major breakthrough came in the early 1950s with the introduction of the bikini.

Such brevity – minimal top, minimal briefs – had never been seen before, and every woman wanted a bikini. The new garment was named for an atoll in the Pacific Ocean's Marshall Islands, which had been the site of atomic bomb tests in 1946. The implication was that the effect of the bikini would be as powerful as that of any atomic blast!

Within two summers the look of beaches all over the world had been transformed as old-style costumes were replaced by bikinis and bodies got their most extensive tans yet.

Today, almost fifty years later, the first bikinis seem almost modest. The briefs have been further abbreviated to little more than a tiny triangle tied in place with thongs or strings, and the top has often been rejected altogether. Nevertheless, some fragment of cloth will always remain, to preserve the mystery.

Bare Essentials

Going topless is the obvious answer to the problem of a tan spoiled by white lines; fortunately social attitudes are now happy to tolerate this maximum-exposure sunbathing, and beaches the world over shelter such golden goddesses.

Bare Essentials

Bare Essentials

On spacious beaches as well as in secluded coves, young women have at last achieved the freedom to enjoy the benefits of sun and sea as unencumbered by clothes as possible.

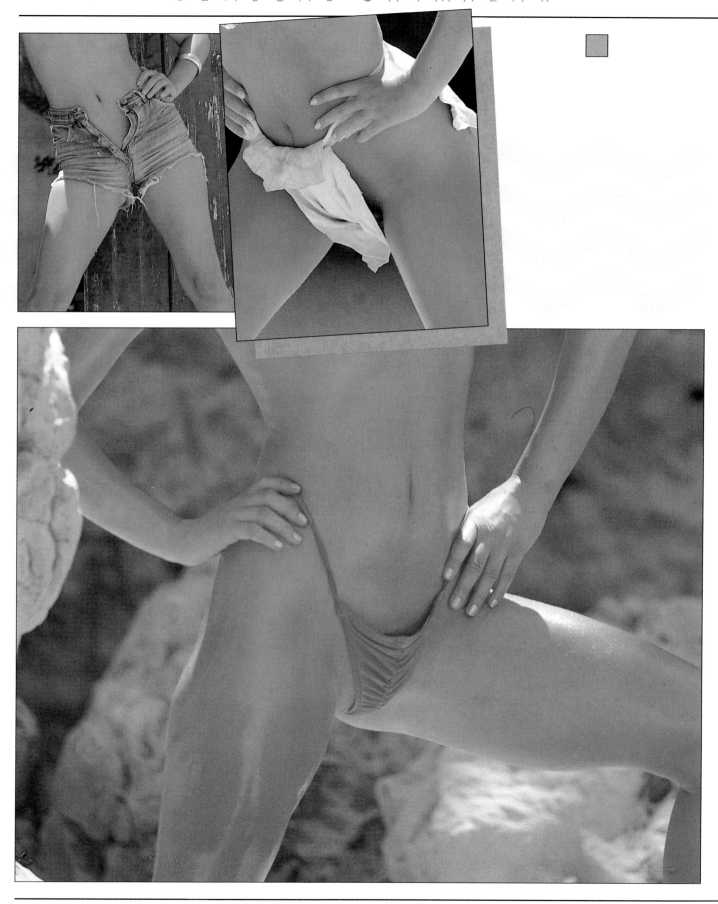

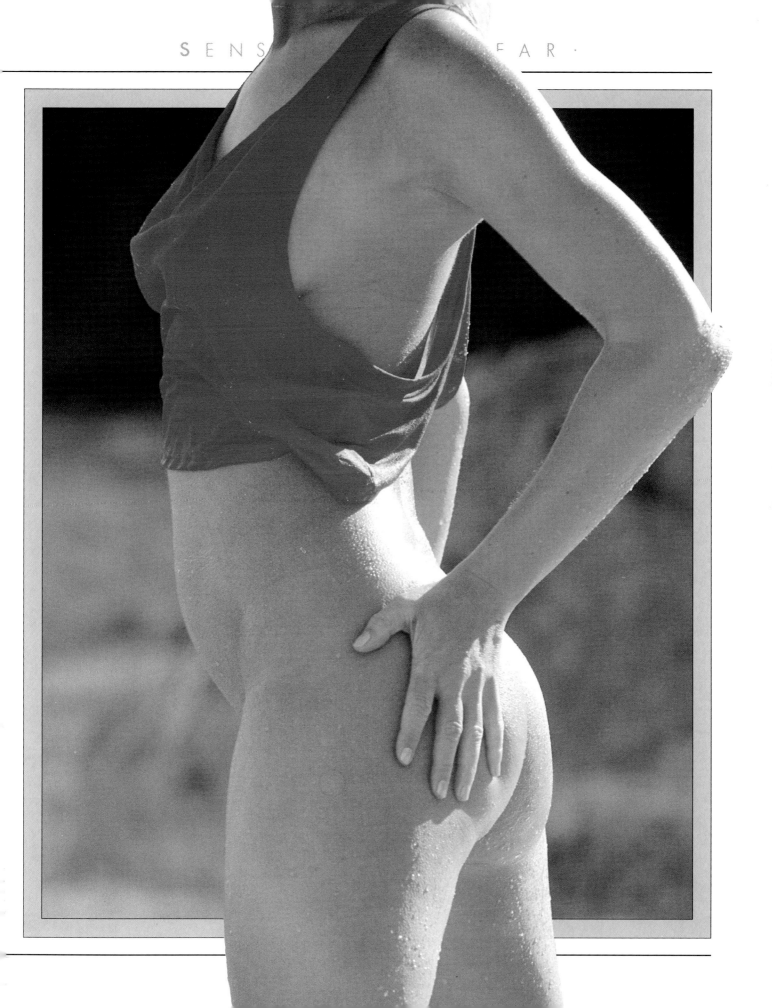

Bare Essentials

Beach girls wear lace; jungle girls wear skins; country girls wear cotton: even the tiniest garment makes a statement, through its color, style and texture, that allows the wearer to stand out from the crowd.

Black and Tanned

Black creates subtle barriers. The woman in black is mysterious, slightly remote, elegant and sophisticated. Although she seems to be saying "Don't approach me," she nevertheless exercises a magnetism few can resist. The girl who chooses to wear a black swimsuit is setting herself apart from the other candy colors on the beach as something extra special.

However, black is not playful; black does not giggle and splash in the shallows or build sandcastles. Black is not gregarious; black lies brooding and silent, a little apart, studying the world through the dark glasses that emphasize the theme. Black is not trivial; black will swim like a dolphin and dive like a cormorant in an impressive display of polished expertise that is individual, self-controlled, and usually faultless.

Black outlines the shape of a tanned body more precisely and more definitely than any other color, emphasizing its sensuality with striking impact. Even in the great outdoors, black retains its sophistication. The picture on page eighty-five may show Ava Gardner stranded on a desert island, but her black lace costume seems to suggest an invitation to visit a suave Fifth Avenue apartment rather than a little straw hut.

Yet if black suggests the indoors rather than the outdoors, it has – perhaps for this very reason – a welcome place by the water, providing contrast and weaving its mysterious spell: even the simplest costume can bring a touch of black magic to the beach.

Black and Tanned

Black and Tanned

Sensual Swimwear

Shaping Up

One of the major changes brought about by the evolution of the swimming costume in the twentieth century has been the transformation of the female shape itself. Greater and greater exposure has prompted changes in standards of beauty, and in people's perception of what is desirable. Right up until the 1920s, the accepted image of an attractive woman included plump arms, a generous bosom, and broad hips. The clothes of the time, with their flowing skirts, corseted waists and padded shoulders managed to both hide and to emphasize these physical characteristics.

It was these very characteristics which did not appeal to the rising generation of active, independent young women. They wanted lithe, athletic bodies, lean hipped and flat chested, to swing them into the new worlds of work, leisure and sport that were opening up for women. Certainly every girl who wanted to wear one of the new, daring swimsuits knew she had to change her shape. So the customization of the twentieth-century female body began. Exercise, diet and sport contributed to the achievement of the new ideal.

For very different reasons, the final decades of the century have seen a great resurgence of this basic need to keep fit, and stay in shape. This has, in turn, produced a different development in the history of swimwear – the popularization of the leotard. This close-fitting but flexible one-piece garment is named for a French acrobat who died in 1870, and has been worn by dancers, acrobats and athletic performers for over a century, only becoming more widely worn in fairly recent years. The leotard's appeal is easy to see – it is an eminently practical garment, whether in the gymnasium or on the beach, but it is also flattering to a body that has been kept in perfect trim. Arguments may rage as to what creates the perfect female body; but the obvious answer is that the well-kept body simply creates itself.

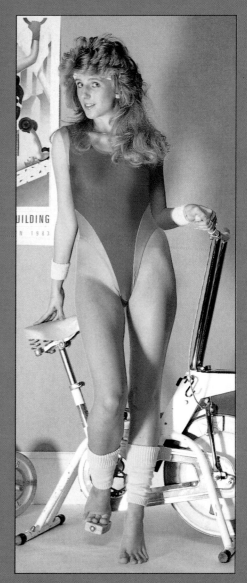

Shaping Up

Shaping Up

White Delight

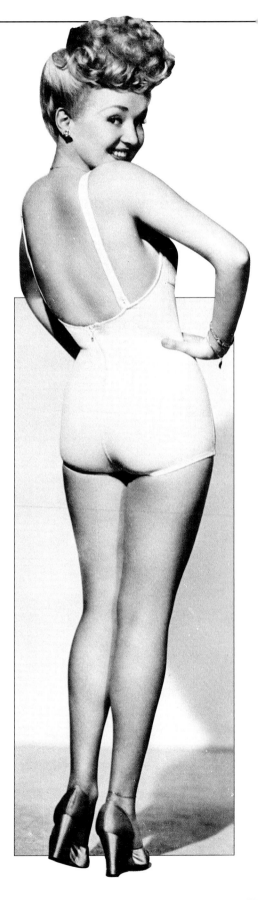

Betty Grable was the pre-eminent pinup girl of the Second World War; sometimes she seemed to have been created specially for the bathing suit and she was photographed in them many hundreds of times. This portrait was certainly her most famous, and it found its way into the tents, ships, planes, and barracks of serving men the world over. Yet it is a very simple shot of an ordinary, if very pretty, girl in a very ordinary swimming costume – there is no attempt at elaborate presentation or spurious glamour.

Grable never aspired either to the high-powered beauty of, say, Rita Hayworth, or to any great acting ability. Her image was that of the girl next door for whom the soldiers were fighting, and who would be there for them to come home to. The bathing costume Grable is wearing fits the image to perfection. In accordance with the demands of the early 1940s, it is modest in cut with a high back and a straight line across the top of the thigh. Its magical touch is that it is white – representing innocence and purity.

This is how white works – it begs no questions, and suggests no ambiguities. The message becomes clear on seeing the stars who are famous for their superb looks in white swimwear. On page ninety-eight, white flatters the celebrated beauty of Raquel Welch and Rita Hayworth, but strips them of complexity.

This message has retained its power over the years and today both the girl next door and the celebrated beauty will still choose white when they wish to project an image of freshness and of uncomplicated simplicity.

White has other advantages: it lends clarity to the outline of a perfect figure and provides the ideal contrast for an exquisitely tanned skin, giving it a burnished glow that no other color can quite manage. The costume may be cut for serious swimming, or it may be as minimal as decency allows; it may have a see-through top, or be completed by shorts or the brief frill of a skirt ... but if it is white, its fresh, uncomplicated message comes across with a sparkling clarity.

White Delight

White Delight

Sensual Swimwear

Costume Jewelry

Jewelry worn with swimwear creates the shock of the unexpected. It seems so inappropriate; after all, jewels go with dressing up for special occasions, and apparently have little to do with the sun, the sea, and the open air. However, the unexpected is also alluring, as sensual women down the ages have recognised. In the 1920s, one of London's most chic women, Mrs. Reginald Fellowes, set the stylistic trends for a new age, breaking established rules and creating her own. One of the things she did which created a stir was to wear her jewelry when dressed for the beach. Far from being a silly piece of ostentation, this, as she well knew, simply added to her glamour. It may have been Mrs. Fellowes whom the painter Kees van Dongen had in mind when he painted his 1924 portrait *The Bather*, depicting a beautiful woman in a swimming costume leaning pensively on a rail. One hand is adorned with a huge diamond ring, while on her arm is a massive, sparkling bracelet.

The effect is frankly sexy and is one that most women seem to know, almost instinctively, how to create. Sometimes a slender gold chain encircling the throat can be more effective than a shower of diamonds; but on a long, exquisitely tanned arm, the hard glitter of that shower of diamonds can contrast beautifully with the tender vulnerability of flesh. Large, hooped earrings in gold or silver give a hint of the dramatic gypsy, while heavy, elaborate collars of wrought metal emphasize the wearer's fragility. Necklaces of coral, shells or shark's teeth have obvious affinities with the sea and their clear colors shine out against a well-tanned skin.

Whatever a woman chooses to wear in the way of swimwear, and whatever aspect of her personality she thereby chooses to express, the gleam of jewelry at ears, throat, wrists, or even ankles, adds the final touch of romantic imagination to the stunning image she has created.

Costume
Jewelry